Inside my mind

AF624545

Joanne Quinn

BookLeaf Publishing

Presentation by *BookLeaf Publishing*

Web: www.bookleafpub.com

E-mail: info@bookleafpub.com

ISBN: 9789357210829

First edition 2022

DEDICATION

To my amazing, unique, sassy, loud, beautiful, quirky, intelligent children and grandchildren.

And to all of you I love.

This one's for you!

ACKNOWLEDGEMENT

For every experience
I have had
Sometimes good
Sometimes bad

All of these
collected here
Written by me
near Wigan Pier

PREFACE

So long have I wanted to write a book.
Always something to get in the way.
By starting on a shorter challenge, whilst using my love of writing poems, here we have 'inside my mind'
I've long used poetry to express my thoughts and feelings. It's seen me throughout many difficult times, but also happiness.
I hope the content shows the variety of my life.

Daddy

I wish I could make
some people 'see'
the same way about things
the same way as me

A person that was once
Was my whole life
Who laughed, who cared
Who made me his wife

That person is gone
The damage is done
But the link is there
You made me a mum

You hurt them
That hurts me
You hurt them again
Why can't you see?

You stupid man
You are a fool
You prance about
You think your cool

Your children should be

the world to you
to care for and pay for
at least while at school

You've failed as a father
I've failed as a mum
I've learnt from my failings
what have you done?

Sat back why I've raised them
and paid not a pound
But watch out Daddy
karma goes round!

Someone

A night, a dream
An endless scream

The smiles the fun
Get out, quick, run

A night to end with blood and tears
Effects to last for many years

The wave of grief to crush and burn
Human choice, we never learn

Someone's Daughter
Someone's Son
Someone's Daddy
Someone's Mum

A tragic date the 22nd
when 22 souls went to heaven
The 23rd in Satan's cell
I hope he rots
In eternal hell

Lend me your soul

Lend me your soul dear Dublin
Let me just rest here a while
The Beauty the culture the people
Provide me an endless smile

Lend me your soul dear Dublin
As I walk down the cobblestone street
Admiring the buildings and culture
Friends with whomever I meet

Lend me your soul dear Dublin
As I stand on the Ha'penny Bridge
Taking in all my surroundings
Wishing this was where I lived

Lend me your soul dear Dublin
As I walk into that bar
The laughter the craic and the music
the best I've encountered so far

Lend me your soul dear Dublin
As I stand on O'Connell street
Remembering the long ago heroes
Too soon their maker did meet

Lend me your soul dear Dublin
I feel I know you so well
I love you my beautiful Dublin
No one can break that spell

My Mum

I can't believe you should be 78 today
If the bloody cancer hadn't taken you away
We missed so much
It still hurts now
I imagine how life
would be different somehow

I'm past the age when you went away
I'm so unlucky
people do say
But to them
my reply would simply be
I'd rather of had you
you were my mum you see

We had 14 short years
I then muggled through
without my mum
what else could I do?

I have my own kids
and grandsons too
They missed out plenty
on a nanny like you
I love them all so very much

I talk about you
and keep them in touch

I'm sure you'd have plenty to say
my choice of men
disastrous but hey..

I've not changed so much
in all that time
I still miss you mum
But I’m glad you were mine.

Mark

We talked of this day
on that last night out
You called me old
as chips flew about
We often talked our different views
When I was in Auchwitz you wanted the news
We had a chat
agreed for a while

But with regards to Ireland
Views differed so much
We both wouldn't listen
and got in a huff

So the day is here
you would of turned forty
You wouldn't of liked it
you'd still of been naughty

Instead you have gone
to the land of the young
were you can look good
and remain still strong

So many to miss you

Life journeys on
In everyone's heart
you've not really gone

So happy 40th Mark
wherever you are
I'll toast to you're birthday
to somewere afar
Here's hoping you know the impact you left
on your loved ones and family
who are still left bereft

But the Mark that I knew
was funny and proud
And would be in Berlin
or a raving crowd

So whichever party
you're spirit is at
enjoy Mr Kenny
and don't be a prat

tir na nOg

Dad

25 years without my Papa Joe
It's gone so fast
I'll have you know

We fought we laughed
we joked and cried
The last conversation
never thought you'd of died

Alone I felt
I still do today
though I kept my promise
As you did say

Along came my Son
Your alike don't you know
Daft as brush
Same as his Grandad Joe

We call him Joey
whom you never met
I wish you had
my big regret!

The Irish songs

the times we've missed
the jokes in the Shammy
And getting pissed!

I shouldn't swear
But it needed saying

I miss you Dad
That is so true
Along with others
we once all knew

The legends that where part of standish
it's not the same
you wouldn't like it!
How much for a pint
I'd imagine you saying
not a ten-pence a pint
like in 1957

Here's mi hand
here's mi heart
I'll love you forever
Forever apart

In the spirit of Joe
the loveable rogue
share us a story a tale or a fight

It's good to remember and keep memories alight

And just one more thing
tonight if you can
when having a toast
remember the Man

My Papa Joe, a long time has passed
it's New Year's Eve so raise up your glass......

Daddy

You were the dad that I once knew
But little do you know the pain I've been
through
I've grown up and seen
That your life is a sham
No room for me
you don't give a damn.

You say that you love me more than I know
But if that were true then why doesn't it show?

I know you have her
you love her I'm sure
But don't forget we are blood
doesn't that mean more?

I remember
I was the twinkle in your eyes.
Then you left one day
without saying goodbye

You say I'm the kid
and other such stuff
but why is spending time with me
never enough?

I'm your daughter
And you're supposed to be my Dad
I feel second place
it makes me feel sad

Does that mean anything to you?
That you'll never see
Your kid on the beach and paddling in the sea

When you are old
and live with regret
you will say sorry
I do expect
But time will have gone
the days turned to years
and nothing left
of my little girl tears

But time moves on
the sadness will fade
Empty promises
never prevail

Dad this is it
this time I'll not try
From this day forward
Though I loved you
Goodbye

Alright

If The pain is hard
If you've lost someone dear
look in your heart
And you'll know they're still here

The flicker of light
The drizzling rain
The bird in the sky
Memories remain

So if you are
struggling through
Just do what you can
what matters
is you

There is no right way
no need to be bright
Keep on going
It will all be alright

I thought of you today

Just a moment today
I thought of you
It happens often
It's nothing new

The what's
The ifs
The whys
The but's

A lifetime has gone
Go on I must

The ache in my heart
Will never go
It hurts still now
But you'd never know

Life moves on
People change
New love appears
Does that seem strange?

I have no regrets
I'd do it again

I'd bypass the split
And bypass the pain

I wish you well
I really do
I hope this time
It's really true

Good luck
God bless
Goodbye
I'm sad but
I won't cry

The time rolls on
Each year it's faster
But this falling in love
I just can't master

I think that love
Has failed the test
It won't return
I tried my best

I'll never have
That lifelong love
Were two entwine
Fit like a glove

I watch and see
My family grow
The best love
that I could know

No regrets
Lessons learned
Chapters written
Pages turned

I miss you

Time together
Time apart
Loving a man
Who breaks your heart

Feeling the rush
When it’s all brand new
Feeling bereft
when he doesn’t call you

Waiting in vain
to make him fall
Living in pain
Your heart so sore

Love can hurt
Like a broken bone
When it falls apart
and your left alone

They say time heels
And maybe it’s true
Some love is forever
I still miss you

Tin man

The tin man
with his broken heart
Loving and leaving
Another new start

The pattern has formed
It will remain
The broken dreams
The lifelong pain

The world has many
Missed connections
broken hearts
And imperfections

The lucky few
Will find their mate
But for the most
A lifelong ache

Protecting with armour
The tin women or men
Falling through life
No Barbie and Ken

Beauty

He leaned on the bars
His arms stretched high

His muscles were pumped
What a beautiful guy

He turned to smile
At his reflection
Knowing full well
He was perfection

He flexed and posed
I was transfixed
I wish I could
take a sneaky pic

He caught my glance
I looked away
I looked again
His eyes had stayed

My stomach flipped
As he walked over
My palms did sweat
For this Casanova

He took my hand
And led me away
Like lamb to the slaughter
The proverbial Prey

No words were spoken
Non were needed
We devoured each other
I did what he did

Into the shower
Naked, exited
Pinned to the tiles
Hormones ignited

Bodies as one
My god he was awesome
Like in slow motion
It went on and then some

The water then stopped
My breathing slowed down
He gave me a smile
This king with his crown

He then walked out
I sank to the floor
Who was this guy

I needed some more

I never did see
His beauty again
But if I did
I would do the same

Friends

What is a friend
A partner in fun
A keeper of secrets
Between us there's none

Someone to support us
through all of life's woes
For nights in or out
Sure anything goes

I would support them
Through thick and thin
Share with their laughter
And never give in

Sadly I think
others don't share
The feelings of honour
They're no longer there

Sad though it's true
Many will fail
To remember your friendship
When it's over a male

Those fair weather friends
I do not need
They do not care
Fuelled by greed

My friends get fewer
As lessons are learned
But the ones still remaining
Your friendship is earned

Holy Joe

Holy Joe made a holy show
When he walked up to that floozie
She wasn't fierce nor was she fine
An ole wagon on the boozie

She smiled at Joe
As she leaned on the wall
As she was fairly langers
Ten euro bud if you wanna cop
of these ole deadly bangers

Joe did blush
his face was scarlet
To be offered that
by this langers Harlot

He thought to leg it
His calling waned
He wasn't used
to life on the game

He offered her blessings
And she did roar
Get out ye money
Or away from mi door

Joe stood still
Not knowing what to say
Where are you God
As the tenner he did pay

Sometimes life
cannot be solved
By a prayer nor by good wishes
But life goes on like days before
with a Molly selling fishes

Hope

Ireland's unique
producer of heroes
The list it is long
some were like nemo

The island of Ireland
A pot of gold
Not always respected
But always bold

The fierce few
The spirit strong
Resilience bred
Unbreakable bond

The Emerald Isle
The language of dreams
split into two
In British made teams

The jury stays out
The country divided
You pick your side
Religion decided

There is no way
This can be sorted
Hope stays on minds
Westminster aborted

The bar

The singers the legends
That this bar has seen
The céilís and laughter
Absorbed in each beam

The drinks and the tales
Many have spilled
The lovers of story's
would be oh so thrilled

To know the history
that these walls hold
When to be quiet
When to be bold

The walls like a shamrock
Lucky if four
Everyday different
who will walk in the door

Some whispers long gone
Some are still here
Life stories spoken
Shared with a beer

History seeped in
each nook and cranny
Songs still sang
about that boyo Danny

Nowhere else
can you have the craic
The fun and the banter
Ensures you'll be back

A stage that many acts pass
To meet there with friends
To just have a gas

Friends not yet met
Songs not yet written
It's deadly in here
We know you'll be smitten

Whatever you seek
You can find here within
So don't be shy
G'wan come on in

The Auld Dub

Tp has
THE best little pub
It's known to locals
as The Auld Dub!

The Craic is plenty
the beer is great
but get in early
It's too good to wait.

We have the honour
of an invite you see
25years owned by Tp
A mighty achievement
We all do agree

But now a line
dedicated to Marie
gone but not forgotten
in the Dubs history
We miss her greatly
everyone does
Her smile and presence
without any fuss

The years have seen
lots of folks pass
but their souls live on
with us and the staff

A fantastic club
we are proud to be part
we love the Auld Dub
with all of our hearts

So raise a glass
to those 25years
of laughter, love
and a sometimes tears!

The Auld Dub
a legend a star
with locals world over
be near or be far

So Tp thank you
for all you have done
here's to the next chapter
With even more fun!

My children

First came Emma
My life then did start
The little dote
My love, my heart

Along came Chloe
My love it did double
Absolute cutey
But sure loving trouble

Next came Sophie
The little quiet one
Sucking her fingers
And watching the fun

Fourth it was Joey
The prodigal son
We nearly lost him
Till the battle was won

Then came Ellie
Last but not least
An ivf miracle
Her twin not to meet

Then after some time
Matthew did wander
Came for his tea
But stayed much longer

My wonderful kids
I could not be more proud
My heart and my soul
But together so loud

Memories I have
From throughout the years
With fun and laughter
And often some tears

My blessings are great
My love it is stronger
Love them forever
But my love will last longer

Theo

My gorgeous Boy
Arrived one year ago
I love him more
than he will ever know

That perfect face
that beaming smile
time doesn't stand still
even for a while

Theo you make my heart burst with pride
my lil man right by my side

Emma and Jamie
what can I say
You have worked so hard
Each wonderful day

I cannot believe
a year's gone so fast
I'd love to pause life
Just make it last

My Baby Girl
with a Baby Boy

My life's complete
Its full of joy

I couldn't imagine
this time last year
How amazing Theo
would be once here

Happy 1st Birthday Theo-James
Happy Birthday to you
I will love even more next year
when you are turning Two

Have a wonderful time
on your holibobs
with Marshall and the other wee Dogs

I'll see you soon for a great big kiss
That little face
I sure will miss

So here's a kiss from Nanny
plus heres a great big hug
My heart always will be
filled with eternal love

Son

Do I love ya? Indeed I do
You're a bleeding nightmare
But my Son, that is true

I often say you're gorgeous
I mean it every word
But you don't want me saying that
You'd say I over shared

A mothers loves forever
Her anguish and worry too
What ever trouble you land in
Ill always help you through

You'll always be my baby boy
No matter how old you are
I love you to the moon and back
Even though you nicked my car

You might not see how loved you are
You sometimes feel left out
But my love for you will never stop
As long as I'm about

Darren

Where would I be
if I wasn't here
If I'd turned a different way
Would life seem more clear

Each choice that we make
Each path that we wander
Takes the journey of life
With no time to ponder

I often think
of the life I might have
If I didn't get in the car
And Darren didn't crash

A decision that changed
My life in a moment
The pain and the injuries
The domino of ailments

We can't change our path
Nor live with regret
We can't mourn the what ifs
Or reset the bet

When times get tough
We wish we could alter
Could go back in time
And not even falter

But this is our life
We must not give in
Live the best you can
Leap the hurdles and grin

www.ingramcontent.com/pod-product-compliance
Lightning Source LLC
Chambersburg PA
CBHW051740130826
49812CB00033B/943
* 9 7 8 9 3 5 7 2 1 0 8 2 9 *